Original title:
Mango Moonlight

Copyright © 2025 Creative Arts Management OÜ
All rights reserved.

Author: Isaac Ravenscroft
ISBN HARDBACK: 978-1-80586-274-1
ISBN PAPERBACK: 978-1-80586-746-3

Embers of Twilight

Under the glow of a silly sky,
Fruits in the trees are all out to fly.
A cheeky breeze starts to sway,
While giggles of laughter stir up the day.

Fuzzy creatures in a waltz take a chance,
Dancing around in a craziest dance.
All the fairies wear hats made of cheese,
Spreading joy like the tiniest breeze.

Stars chuckle as they blink in delight,
Chasing shadows, they join in the night.
With whispers of joy, they tickle the air,
Gathering tales of the night's silly fair.

As shadows grow long, the fun only trills,
With ticklish glee and whimsical thrills.
A scene so bright it lights up the dark,
In the heart of night, there's always a spark.

A Ballet of Twilight Flavors

In a garden where giggles bloom wide,
Fruits spin dervishes, filled with pride.
The sun takes a bow, with a wink of its eye,
While butterflies dance, oh my, oh my!

Lemonade rivers flow in sweet streams,
As jellies wear hats made of whipped cream.
Jesters with spoons dive headlong in,
In a chase for the treats, let the fun begin!

What's that? A fruit with a bubbly surprise,
It plays peek-a-boo, oh what a disguise!
It teases the tongue with flavors so bright,
Making everyone giggle with pure delight.

As the curtain of night draws the day to a close,
Each laugh and each cheer beautifully flows.
In the lingering light where the giggles collide,
A ballet of flavors, with joy as our guide!

Moonlit Orchard Paths

Under the glow of a round, bright orb,
Ripe surprises await, in fruit we absorb.
Whispers of laughter dance through the trees,
As critters snack on sweet treats with ease.

Silly shadows leap on the ground,
While fruity aromas swirl all around.
A raccoon steals a berry, wearing a hat,
Twirling under the stars, how about that!

Citrus Caress

In the hum of the night, a zesty affair,
Lemons laugh loudly, while limes steal a stare.
Oranges giggle as they roll down the hill,
Tangerines tango with a citrus-filled thrill.

A parrot in disguise cracks jokes with delight,
He juggles fresh fruit in the cool, breezy night.
While laughter erupts from a tree filled with cheer,
This realm of delight is just waiting right here.

Midnight Petals

Frolicsome blooms in a twilight dream,
Tickle the air with their scent, like ice cream.
Petals play peek-a-boo beneath the stars,
With giggling bees buzzing near, oh how bizarre!

Fireflies waltz in a swirling array,
While blossoms gossip about who'll sway.
A flower in pink wears a comical frown,
Saying, 'Why's that bee wearing a tiny crown?'

Glistening Night Blooms

In velvety nights, where the mischief unfolds,
Crickets tell tales of bravado and bolds.
Each petal shines bright, dewy and spry,
While the moon rolls its eyes at the chaos nearby.

Lilacs burst out in a fib about pies,
While orchids perform their best 'wearing disguise.'
Laughter erupts from the garden's delight,
As flowers chop dreams into bits of pure light.

Lunar Tides

When the moon is round and bright,
The fruit bats have a funny flight.
They dip and dive, oh what a sight,
As laughter echoes in the night.

With every wave, the shadows dance,
A lizard waiting for its chance.
It jumps for joy in moonbeam pants,
While crickets play their midnight romance.

Fruits of the Midnight Sky

Under stars that giggle and glow,
The apples plan a cheeky show.
With cherry laughs, they steal the flow,
While bananas dance in line below.

A pineapple dons a tiny hat,
Perched atop a chubby cat.
They sway and twirl, imagine that!
As everyone joins in for a chat.

Illuminated Orchards

In orchards bright with playful beams,
The pears conspire to bash their dreams.
They giggle, wiggle, bursting seams,
While dreaming of their juiciest teams.

A comical crew of citrus cheer,
Declares their zest to spread good cheer.
They juggle fruits till skies are clear,
With funny jokes that all can hear.

Stars Above the Orchard

The stars above play peek-a-boo,
While grapefruits toss a wobble or two.
A melon jokes, 'Can I join you?'
As laughter rolls like morning dew.

Together, they plan a midnight feast,
With giggles shared from west to east.
The night grows bright, their smiles increased,\nAs fruity fun is never ceased.

Evening's Juicy Delight

Under the tree, we swing and sway,
A fruit so sweet, come join the play.
With laughter loud, we take a bite,
Juices drip down, a funny sight.

Friends all gather, the sun slips low,
Sticky fingers start the show.
We toss the pits; oh, what a game,
Laughter echoes, we're all to blame.

Serenade of Golden Glow

The glow of dusk, like butter spread,
We jammed the picnic, now time for bread.
The fruit is ripe, the humor's ripe,
Who knew this feast was such a type?

We giggle loud, we munch and crunch,
The silliness, it's quite a punch.
A dance with fruit, a jiggly twist,
Who knew that supper could be this missed?

Dancing in the Nightshade

Twilight whispers with a giggle,
The fruits on our plates start to wiggle.
With each small bite, a burst of cheer,
We sway with shadows, never fear.

Our jokes take flight like fireflies,
Sticky fingers and joyful sighs.
We dance in circles, a fruity ballet,
Spinning and laughing at the end of the day.

Celestial Ambrosia

Under the stars, we share a feast,
Sweet munchies do make us the least.
With juice-soaked shirts, we laugh aloud,
Our sticky mishap, we're very proud.

The night grows bright with our silly games,
Pits like confetti, it's all the same.
With every bite, the silly grows,
Unforgettable night, everyone knows.

Gleaming Groves

In the grove where shadows play,
Fruitful echoes laugh and sway.
Buddies dance on leafy floors,
Dropping snacks as laughter roars.

Glowing orbs hang from the trees,
Whispering jokes on the breeze.
Silly critters join the show,
Rolling 'round like they don't know.

Breezy whispers, cheeky tunes,
Jovial antics 'neath the moons.
Even branches jig and jive,
While the summer nights arrive.

In this land of giggles bright,
Where the fruits just take to flight.
Every bite a chuckle, too,
Sticky fingers laugh anew.

Serenading the Stars

Underneath the twinkling skies,
Fruits do sing with goofy sighs.
Joke-filled air, the taste of cheer,
Crickets laugh, as friends draw near.

Giggling shadows, fruit galore,
Tickled leaves in playful lore.
Banter floats like sweet perfume,
Joining in the night's grand zoom.

As the stars toss winks and grins,
All the laughter softly spins.
Smiles ripple in the air,
Singeing jokes without a care.

Every bite holds jest so sweet,
Beneath the sky, the night's elite.
With every grin and silly cheer,
An eternal bond draws near.

Lantern of the Tropics

Nights aglow with giggles bright,
Fruits parade in beams of light.
Chasing dreams, the laughter flows,
Elfin sprites in silly clothes.

Swinging lanterns, wild and free,
Every flicker bends the glee.
Fruit juice rivers, sticky streams,
Enchant the heart with joyous dreams.

Creatures join in playful spree,
Bouncing under every tree.
Chirping tales and bubbling cheer,
Life's a party, never fear.

In this land where jesters roam,
Find a friend and make it home.
With every wink, a tale unfurls,
Underneath the glowing swirls.

Elysian Evening

In the dusk where laughter sings,
Fruits play tricks with sticky strings.
Chubby cheeks and twinkled eyes,
Underneath the moonlit skies.

Hopping critters steal the scene,
Zooming past in jestful sheen.
Every shadow hides a grin,
Laughter's dance begins to spin.

Nighttime tales of silly dreams,
Echo through the laughing streams.
Swirling breezes carry sound,
Joyful gigs abound all around.

So gather round, embrace the cheer,
In this paradise, all is clear.
With fun and fruits, the night's aglow,
Elysian moments steal the show.

Fragrant Echoes

In the garden, fruits do sway,
The mischievous breeze pipes away,
A sweet aroma fills the air,
Critters twirl without a care.

Bumbles dance on candy trails,
While laughter loops in happy gales,
Even squirrels wear silly hats,
As night falls, look, a cat that chats!

Sublime Summer Nights

Stars are plump like jellybeans,
Glow in skies of ice cream dreams,
Crickets sing a quirky tune,
While fireflies flash like spoons.

A raccoon steals the picnic spread,
With jammy paws and crumbs to shred,
The moon grins down on all the fun,
In this wild game, no one has won!

Caramelized Skies

The skies drip sweet with creamy hues,
As you dodge the sticky goo,
A paper boat floats down the stream,
Adventurers chase a gooey dream.

Grins are stuck like sticky notes,
The laughter floats, our little boats,
We glide on smiles, oh what a stir,
Until we trip on jammed-up fur!

Essence of Dawn

Morning peeks with a wink so sly,
As sleepy heads begin to fly,
A rooster crows, but misses the beat,
And lands it awkwardly on his feet.

With toast in hand and thoughts a-flutter,
We laugh at birds who seem to stutter,
While sunrise spills like melted cheese,
Another day of silly tease!

Celestial Bounty

Under the stars, in a glow,
Laughter drips, like juice, you know.
Fruits swing low, oh what a sight,
We dance in the shadows of lunar light.

Giggles bounce as we weave and dart,
Caught in the web of a fruity heart.
A twinkle here, a chuckle there,
As sweetness tickles, it fills the air.

The night is ripe with fruity cheer,
Filled with laughter, we shed a tear.
One too many, we start to sway,
The cosmos giggles, come join the play.

With every bite, the night grows light,
We burst in joy, oh what a sight!
In jovial circles, we sip and feast,
Under the stars, we're never ceased.

Glisten of the Night Fruit

In the glow of heaven's tease,
We munch away with such great ease.
Fruits of laughter, gleam like gold,
Stories of mischief silently told.

Stars blink down with a knowing grin,
As we take bites, our heads spin.
Juice runs down, it's quite the sight,
We giggle under the sparkling night.

A fruit fight breaks, the crowd goes wild,
We're all just kids, the cosmos smiled.
With every squirt, our spirits soar,
In the fruity frenzy, we want more!

Spare no bite, let's raise a cheer,
In this night's banquet, there's nothing to fear.
Together we feast, the universe sings,
In absurdity found, oh what joy it brings!

Whimsy Under the Stars

In the twilight, we take our seat,
Adventures await, all ripe and sweet.
We riddle the night with giggles and grins,
As the fruit dance begins, let's spin and spin.

Laughter echoes as we trip and slide,
Orange peels, we throw with pride.
Stars are watching, or so we claim,
In our fruit-filled frolic, we play a game.

Juicy bites and a sugary swirl,
As our laughter keeps on to twirl.
Caught in chaos, we cheer and shout,
Under the cosmic laugh, there's never doubt.

So let the night be our silly friend,
Where sweetness blooms, and fun won't end.
We laugh 'til dawn, under bright skies,
In this joyous romp, we fly so high.

Chasing Celestial Flavors

Up in the sky, where stars do sway,
We hunt for taste in a quirky way.
With fruity dreams sprouting wide,
Beneath the cosmos, we laugh and glide.

Whispers of flavors in the night breeze,
Caught in the whimsy, with such ease.
Each bite ignites a joyful song,
As we dance with twinkles, oh how we throng!

Silly faces and sticky hands,
Sprinting wildly through vibrant lands.
As sweetness bursts, we hold our sides,
In delight, the universe abides.

So lift your glass to the fruity delight,
Let joy reign supreme in the soft night light.
With every chuckle, every cheer, we find,
The cosmic humor, so sweet, so kind.

Fruitful Melodies

In a grove where laughter grows,
The trees wear hats, the fruit in rows.
Bananas slip on socks to dance,
While apples try to steal a glance.

A pear with shades is quite the sight,
As cherries giggle through the night.
They sing a tune of juicy cheer,
Inviting all to join the sphere.

Each berry jumps with glee and flair,
While lemons juggle in fresh air.
The rhythms twist, the fun unfolds,
In fruity tales that joy beholds.

So come and sway beneath the glow,
Of sweetened dreams that fruits bestow.
Embrace the tunes that nature plays,
In merry moods of sunny days.

Lustrous Horizon

On the edge of dusk, the skies ignite,
With giggles of the stars not quite polite.
They gossip of a grapefruit's pride,
While oranges roll down for a slide.

Watermelons dance in vibrant hues,
As pineapples wear funny shoes.
The horizon's painted with laughter's light,
A canvas bright, oh what a sight!

Lemons play tag with the zesty breeze,
While coconuts sway on swaying trees.
The sun dips shy, but fruit's aglow,
As shadows play hide and seek below.

In this horizon where giggles bloom,
Fruits charm the earth, they chase the gloom.
With every twinkle, the joy expands,
In playful hearts, the laughter stands.

Sunkissed Reflections

The sun peeks in, a curious eye,
On a pear-shaped cheek, it passes by.
Reflections giggle in the pond,
As grapefruits float and dance beyond.

A cheeky peach with a fluffy hug,
Cracks a joke, gives the sun a shrug.
Bouncing berries race in pairs,
As the daffodils lend their cares.

Honeydew dreams on water's edge,
Rippling round like a playful pledge.
They weave and swirl with fruity flair,
In sunlit joy, none would despair.

As the sun sets, the laughter stays,
In sunkissed hues of golden rays.
Reflections wrap the world in fun,
As evening lands, a day well done.

Sweet Citrus Reverie

In a realm where zest dreams rise,
Citrus curls up under skies.
A tangerine wears a cozy hat,
While lemons chat about the cat.

With giggles fresh and tangy spring,
Oranges dream of a fancy fling.
They spin and twirl with merry ease,
As zestful breezes tease the trees.

A clementine sings a silly song,
While limes play tag, it won't be long.
The fruity jive, a sweet escape,
Where every peel forms a new shape.

As night falls, their laughter glows,
In citrus tones, the joy bestows.
A reverie so bright and sweet,
In every flavor, the fun's complete.

Crescent Shadows

In the garden, fruit takes a chance,
Squirrels waltz in a silly dance.
Laughter echoes 'neath a starry sky,
As cats chase fireflies that seem to fly.

Lemons giggle from the citrus tree,
While limes hide away, oh so sprightly!
We chase each other, all in good fun,
As the moon plays peek-a-boo with the sun.

Up above, the crescent grins wide,
The night is ours; there's joy to confide.
Juggling stars, we keep the pace,
Who knew the night could be such a race?

With every laugh, our hearts take flight,
As shadows grow beneath the light.
Let's feast on dreams, oh, what a sight,
In the glow of the fruit named for delight.

Midnight Harvest

Underneath the gleaming sky,
We gather fruits, oh my, oh my!
Tummy tickles from all the pranks,
Sneaky squirrels slink to the banks.

Chasing shadows, dodging the breeze,
Brilliant oranges among the leaves.
We giggle loud to scare away fears,
While the moon chuckles through the years.

In the orchard, we'll make a mess,
Climbing trees, oh what a stress!
But with each slip, and every fall,
We burst into laughter, that's the call.

So come join this midnight spree,
Where fruits and fun grow endlessly.
We'll create memories, oh what a cast,
In the harvest of laughs that forever last.

Citrus Dreams

Dreams float in the air with zest,
As oranges dress in their Sunday best.
Lemonade rivers flow with cheer,
While giggles bounce round, drawing near.

In a hammock, we swing and sway,
Counting stars at the end of the day.
Citrus kisses in the summer breeze,
With each burst of laughter, life feels at ease.

Oh, the mischief that we can breed,
Chasing shadows, planting seed.
Our dreams are sweet, with a funny twist,
In a world where nothing could be missed.

So gather 'round, let's share this glee,
With fruits and fun, just you and me.
In citrus dreams, laughter reigns true,
In the glow of a world that feels brand new.

Whispers of the Evening Breeze

Under the trees, the secrets lay,
Fruitful whispers at the close of day.
The breeze tells tales of the silly and spry,
While our silly antics cause the stars to cry.

We giggle in shadows, chasing the light,
Turning drab evenings oh so bright.
With every breeze, a chuckle escapes,
Unraveling laughter with funny shapes.

The fruits join in with their own parade,
Chanting joy in a fruity charade.
Under the stars, we toast to delight,
As the moon joins in, what a tasty sight!

Let's dance with the whispering winds, you and me,
Gathering giggles like honey from bees.
Evening laughs, where friendships grow,
In the breeze that tickles, we steal the show.

The Soft Dance of Fruit and Sky

Beneath the tree, a fruit so bold,
It winks at stars, its stories told.
A squirrel twirls with a fruity cheer,
Inviting all to dance with glee.

A breeze floats by with a giggly sigh,
Making the branches sway and fly.
The fruit drops down in a plump, loud thud,
And rolls away like a playful bud.

Laughter echoes as the shadows play,
Crickets sing the night away.
The moon peeks through a leafy veil,
While fruit and fun set out to sail.

So raise a toast to the juicy night,
Where laughter and fruit take sudden flight.
In the grand ballet of tree and air,
Life's a joke—let's dance without a care!

Glowing Fantasies at Dusk

As the sun dips down, so bright and bold,
The fruits all shimmer, in colors gold.
A cheeky parrot starts to squawk,
While we trip over a moonlit rock.

The night is ripe with fuzzy dreams,
The fruit laughs softly as it beams.
Fireflies join in a twisty race,
Illuminating each silly face.

Chasing shadows, we leap and glide,
A parade of giggles, side by side.
The tangy scent fills the merry air,
As we dance like no one's there.

With every bounce, we break the rules,
Turning ripe fruit into playful jewels.
And as the stars begin to cheer,
We find our joy, the night is clear!

Tropical Whispers

In the thick of night, the giggle spreads,
Where fruit hangs low, and all misleads.
A playful breeze pulls at your shirt,
Making you twirl in the soft, sweet dirt.

Beneath the palms, there's wobbly fun,
As coconuts roll and the games begun.
The night air smells of berry and rhyme,
As we slip and slide, oh what a time!

We stumble through shadows, laughter loud,
Creating a scene that's quite the crowd.
With thieves of fruit as our merry crew,
We dance under stars, oh, what a view!

Then suddenly there's a squirt and a pop,
A juicy surprise makes the laughter stop.
Then just like that, the fun resumes,
As we pickle the night in fruity fumes!

Golden Nightfall

The glow of dusk sets the scene just right,
Where goofy fruits twinkle in twilight.
As if on cue, the laughter starts,
With fruity jests that twine our hearts.

A cat named Paws joins the dancing spree,
Chasing after shadows, wild and free.
With every leap, he stumbles and grins,
While the fruit chuckles at his silly spins.

In the distance, drums begin to play,
Inviting all to laugh and sway.
The golden fruits sway to the beat,
As we shuffle along with dancing feet.

So let's make merry till the morning light,
With giggles and fruits feeling oh so right.
For every drop, a laugh shall bloom,
In the golden embrace of the evening's room!

Romance in the Haze

Underneath the glowing sphere,
Two lovers share a sticky cheer.
With fruits that dangle from the trees,
They giggle soft in summer's breeze.

A kiss is sweet as summer's treat,
But juice drips down, oh what a feat!
With laughter loud, they dance around,
As sticky hands and hearts are found.

The grass is green, the fruit's a dream,
And ants parade, they join the scheme.
In every bite, a sparkle bright,
The world is whirling in delight.

So here they sit, both lost in bliss,
With every plop and every kiss.
As mango madness fills the air,
One last sweet hug, without a care.

Ethereal Citrus

In twilight's glow, two friends collide,
With zesty laughs, they chose to ride.
On paths of juice, they slip and slide,
    As tangy dreams begin to bide.

A fruit fight sparked, what a grand scene,
A slice here, a pulp there, oh what cuisine!
They dance with zest and shriek with glee,
    As citrus rain falls from the tree.

With every squirt, a silly prank,
They roll in laughter, no need to thank.
The juice a treasure, sweet as sin,
    In a world where the fun begins.

For in this spilled and cheerful mess,
Life's little laughs are nonetheless.
As night unfolds, their spirits soar,
    Wading in juice, forevermore.

Liquid Gold Beneath the Stars

Beneath the bright and shining night,
They sip from cups of golden light.
The stars above, they twinkle sly,
While fruity laughter fills the sky.

Each drop a giggle, each sip a cheer,
With careless glee, they hold it near.
A toast to all the juicy fun,
As moonbeams dance, they start to run.

Ideas sprout like trees in bloom,
As giggles chase away the gloom.
With every gulp, horizons blend,
While fruity dreams refuse to end.

So here's to nights of pure delight,
With friends who make the stars ignite.
In liquid gold, their joy takes flight,
With memories shimmering, oh so bright.

Mystery of the Night Orchard

In shadows deep, they wander wide,
Among the trees, where secrets hide.
With giggles soft and whispered plans,
They reach for fruit with eager hands.

A crunch, a munch, what could it be?
The taste of fun held in esprit.
With masks of juice, they slip and slide,
As laughter echoes through the night.

Each bite unveils a tale untold,
Of evenings spent in glistening gold.
With winks and whispers, they devise,
A game of fruit beneath the skies.

So let them roam in playful glee,
In orchards filled with mystery.
For every laugh, a tale is spun,
In a world of fruits, their hearts are won.

Savory Serenade

Under the sky so bright and wide,
Fruits dance with joy, they take a slide.
A banana jig, a grapey spin,
While lemons laugh, and oranges grin.

Peaches whisper to the shy old pear,
'Come join the fun, we're quite the pair!'
Even the limes can't hide their glee,
As cherries cheer with sweet jubilee.

Pineapples play tag, what a game!
While berries tumble, oh what a fame!
Under the stars, they bust a move,
Grooving in rhythm, superbly smooth.

Dancing under the silver glow,
A fruity fiesta, don't be slow!
Join the ruckus, let laughter ring,
In this delightful soirée of zing.

Harvest Moon's Embrace

Beneath the orb of shimmering light,
Fruits whisper secrets, oh what a sight!
An apple giggles, a kiwi jests,
As they lounge about in leafy vests.

The pumpkin shimmies, with golden flair,
While melons tell tales of summer air.
Grapes drop puns, as peaches chime in,
In this fruity frolic, let the fun begin.

Under the harvest, they plop and sway,
Bouncing and jouncing throughout the day.
With laughter erupting in juicy pools,
Who knew such fun could break all the rules?

Each fruit a character, lively and bright,
Hosting a gala under the night.
With every giggle, the shadows lean,
In this sweet party, a whimsical scene.

Nightfall Nectar

When dusk creeps in and giggles grow,
Fruits come out to steal the show.
A zesty lime wears a jazzy hat,
While cherries chatter, having a spat.

Bananas balance on top of peels,
Kumquats tumble, how good it feels!
The night air is filled with ripe delight,
As berries break into a dance so right.

Lemons chuckle at the awkward pear,
Who tripped on grass, oh what a scare!
The pomegranates cheer, delightedly loud,
As the fruits form a wobbly parade crowd.

Under the stars, they sway to the tune,
With laughter echoing, bright as a balloon.
In a fruity frenzy, they welcome the night,
As joy spills forth in pure delight.

Luminous Grove

In a grove aglow with a vibrant glow,
Fruits trade jokes, putting on quite a show.
A walnut cracks wise, a peach takes the mic,
While cantaloupe sings out in real hike.

Grapefruit grins as it starts to sway,
Peppers look on, "Hey, join the fray!"
With every joke, the fun escalates,
As apples throw pies, and laughter mandates.

The pranks unfold in the moon's soft gaze,
Carrots and cucumbers join in the craze.
Berries giggle, weaving tales of cheer,
In this luminous grove, we dance without fear.

As twilight beckons, the laughter persists,
Fruits unite in an evening twist.
In this jovial realm of playful delight,
The grove stands alive, sparkling bright.

Amber Skies

In the golden glow, the fruit stands tall,
Laughter spills from the trees, a juicy brawl.
Squirrels dance, their tails a blur,
Chasing dreams, they giggle and stir.

Beneath the beams, the air's so sweet,
A sticky snack makes for a treat.
Frogs serenade in a quirky croak,
Even the brook seems to crack a joke.

Fireflies waltz in their tiny suits,
While the moon grins down at the fruity hoots.
A group of ants line up, so neat,
Planning a feast for an unexpected meet.

In this twilight, laughter soars,
A zany world with open doors.
Friends gather 'round with silly cheer,
In the glow of the night, there's nothing to fear.

Celestial Citrus

A ball of zest hangs, bursting bright,
Witty whispers flow through the night.
The breeze chuckles, tickling my nose,
As citrusy glee in the atmosphere grows.

Grape-sized wishes bounce on high,
While clouds throw a party in the sky.
Drunk on joy, the stars take flight,
Sipping on dreams 'til the morning light.

Crickets compose a jolly tune,
Tap-dancing under the cheeky moon.
Oh, what a night for laughter sweet,
As flavors collide in a fun, twirly beat.

Under the glow, let whimsy reign,
With giggles and grins that need no gain.
In this cosmic fun, we'll take our place,
With cheer and zest in a floating embrace.

Starlit Eden

In a garden of dreams, the night unfolds,
Where chuckles flutter like stories untold.
Giggling daisies dance in the light,
As petals share secrets, taking flight.

Bubbles of joy float past the fence,
And laughter bounces in rhythmic suspense.
Crickets spread tales with a comedic flair,
While moonbeams tickle the soft, warm air.

Amidst the leaves, a skit takes shape,
With frogs in top hats, escaping the drape.
They hop and they croon, what an odd sight,
In this paradise, everything feels right.

So in this Eden, let fun reside,
With silly antics my heart cannot hide.
As night wears on, we'll sparkle and spin,
Where golden giggles make the world grin.

Savoring the Night Breeze

The night breeze whispers hilarious tales,
Of creatures that wear the silliest veils.
An owl in glasses reads the stars,
While a cat brags of his shining cars.

Beneath the glow, shadows play chess,
Each move met with giggles, no need to impress.
A funny breeze, it teases my hair,
With ticklish giggles floating in the air.

The harvest moon, a playful guide,
Lights up the night like a joyous slide.
We chase after dreams, wild and free,
In this carnival of whimsy, come dance with me.

Oh, to savor the breezes so light,
Where laughter ignites in the calm of night.
Together we bask in this cheerful spree,
In the jolly embrace of nature's decree.

Tropical Whispers

In the warm glow of night, a dance begins,
With fruits in the air, where the silliness spins.
A parrot squawks jokes, with a wink of delight,
While coconuts giggle, embracing the night.

Swaying palms chuckle, their shadows all quirk,
As the night creeps on, there's no sign of work.
Bananas put on hats, a party they seek,
And limes roll around, with legs growing weak.

Fragrant breezes carry a laughter-filled tune,
As guavas groove gently, beneath a bright moon.
An octopus juggles, with eight arms of cheer,
Laughing all night, not a worry in here.

In the tropical air, joy takes its flight,
With fruits that frolic, oh what a sight!
So join in the fun, let your spirit unfurl,
In this nighttime carnival, come dance and twirl!

Nocturnal Harvest

Under a sky where the stars are a tease,
Fruits hang low, dancing, as light sets the breeze.
A turtle in shades shuffles over to peek,
While rabbits tell secrets, their laughter unique.

With vines overgrown, tomatoes wear frowns,
They envy the chutneys and sweet summer gowns.
Beans burst out laughing, as carrots do strut,
While onions just cry and potato hugs butt.

The moon spins around like a cheeky old chap,
As berries unite for an impromptu clap.
Outrageous debates on who's juiciest, best,
While squash sneaks a kiss from a star at their fest.

In this carnival scene, all veggies unite,
For laughter and stories beneath the moonlight.
So harvest your joy, it's ripe for the take,
In this nocturnal show, for goodness' sake!

Luminous Nectar

In a land where the fruit salads dance on the breeze,
Lemons wear hats as the mangoes say cheese.
The sun dips away, yet the fun's just begun,
With apples in laughter, as round as they run.

Under a canopy, night jokes abound,
While fruits play charades, giggling all around.
A pineapple juggles, oh what a great plight,
As cherries get tipsy, igniting the night!

Papaya and guava share stories of fun,
With dates throwing shade at the sleepy old sun.
Beneath the green leaves, in shadows they thrive,
A crazy fruit party, let's hope they survive!

With raucous cheer rolling, it's hard to ignore,
As nature's finest take the stage, they encore.
So sway to the rhythm, let laughter ignite,
In the land of the fruit, where dreams are so bright!

Golden Dreams Under Stars

Stars twinkle and shine on the juicy delight,
As lemons and oranges have a fruity fight.
They toss all their zest in a sparkling show,
While plums dance the tango, and mangos say "Whoa!"

The dawn sighs with giggles, as fruit hats depart,
Where apples recite their illustrious art.
A coconut cracks up with friends in a stack,
And pears pie fight, but they never look back!

Under the cosmos, where mysteries lie,
A grape rolls a story that's wickedly sly.
With walnuts in wigs and a party that's grand,
Life is a banquet, come join this sweet band!

So gather, dear friends, in this playful sphere,
Where laughter is golden, and fun disappears.
Under diamond skies, let joy take its course,
In nature's own jester, we find our true source!

Shadows of the Citrus Tree

In the garden where laughter sings,
A fruit with a smile, on bright springs.
The squirrels dance, they're quite the show,
With a twirl and a spin, oh what a go!

The breeze whispers jokes through the leaves,
While butterflies giggle, as the sun weaves.
Ladybugs laugh, a comedic crew,
Tickling the branches, just for a view.

When night falls, there's mischief in air,
The fruits wear masks, with a comical flair.
Under the cloak of shadows, they play,
Telling sweet tales that drift far away.

And as stars peek from the twilight dome,
The laughter turns ripe, they feel at home.
Nature's jesters, so witty and bright,
Bring joy and chuckles in the gentle night.

Rays in the Dusk

Golden lights flicker, a playful tease,
As the sun waves goodnight through the trees.
Crickets start crooning, a catchy tune,
While shadows stretch long, beneath the moon.

A parade of fruits, with giggles abound,
Wobbling and jiggling all around.
One slips on a leaf, a hilarious fall,
The others all roar, they can't help but call!

The stars join the fun, they twinkle and blush,
As fireflies join in with a cheerful rush.
Glow-worms are judges, with their sparkling view,
Rating the comics for their funny debut.

In this dusk theater, where laughter ignites,
Citrus comedians steal the bright nights.
With puns on their peels and jokes in their core,
They keep us laughing, always wanting more.

Nectar of the Night

The moon's soft glow turns the scene just right,
As critters convene for their giggling delight.
Buzzing and bubbling, they gather around,
With juicy tales that are quite profound.

The bees bumble in, with a joke or two,
Claiming they're clever, but who really knew?
They stumble and tumble on petals tonight,
Spilling their nectar with blurry flight.

As shadows grow long, a ticklish breeze,
Carries the laughter through the lush trees.
Even the owls with their wise old charms,
Can't help but chuckle at the fruity alarms.

So toast to the night, with a giggly cheer,
For every sweet drop brings humor near.
In the fields where the laughter is made,
Even the moonlight's sting starts to fade.

Orb of Radiance

With a glimmer and glow, the orb takes flight,
Whispering riddles that dance in the night.
Its citrusy charm, a radiant sight,
Bringing zest to the dark, what pure delight!

A troupe of shadows join in the fun,
Chasing each other till the night's nearly done.
Moonbeams reflect on a fruit's shiny skin,
Making it twinkle like a giggling grin.

Squirrels wear capes, as the laughter flows,
While frogs in the pond strike comical poses.
The glow from above adds spark to the jest,
Creating a carnival, it's simply the best!

So let's raise our cups to the stellar display,
With snacks that elicit hilarious play.
For under this orb, where the funny takes flight,
We revel in joy, 'neath the sparkling night.

Savoring the Celestial Blend

Under the stars with a grin so wide,
Munching on fruit, what a joyride!
The sky spills juice, bright and sweet,
As laughter flows with every tasty treat.

Birds in the trees sing tunes so bright,
While squirrels join in, quite the sight!
We'll dance in shadows, twirling around,
With sticky fingers, joy unbound.

A fruit here, a giggle there,
Who knew a night could be so rare?
Each bite's a melody, a playful tease,
Happiness drips like honeyed breeze.

So let's toast under the fruity hue,
To sweet moments, and silly too!
As the night rolls on, let worries flee,
In this celestial feast, we are truly free!

Night Blooms with Tropical Light

The moon winks bright with a cheeky glow,
While critters below put on a show.
Fruit-shaped hats on our heads so proud,
Laughter erupts, oh, we're quite loud!

Fireflies buzzing their glowing jokes,
As we trade quips with the cheeky folks.
Under this canopy of glittery cheer,
Who knew a night could feel so near?

Chill fruits jive with the stars above,
Dancing silly, feeling the love.
Each silly face, a fruity surprise,
In every giggle, our worries die.

So let's sip juice like royal kings,
While nature giggles and sweetly sings.
In the light of the night, we'll thrive and play,
With echoes of fun in our hearts, hooray!

Twilight's Bounty Awaited

As dusk descends with a playful twist,
We gather ripe treasures, can't resist.
Balls of sweetness scatter 'round,
Each flavor bursting, joy profound.

Giggly ghosts hide in leafy shade,
While we feast till the twinkle parade.
With each slice, a goofy grin,
Who knew snacking could feel like a win?

In this twilight of mishap and cheer,
Every little stumble brings laughter near.
Let's make a toast to our silly spree,
For the best bites are always free!

So wedge your worries between the fun,
As our fruity feast comes undone.
Under this sky, we'll laugh in delight,
For every moment shines oh so bright!

Aromas of Dusk's Delight

The scent of adventure floats in the air,
We open the feast, with little care.
Splatters of nectar, are you ready?
Let's dive in deep, just hold steady!

Each giggle rises like pies in the night,
With every good bite, we feel so right.
Squirrels are spying, with mischievous eyes,
Wondering just how we'll claim the prize.

The night hums softly with sizzling fun,
Under this canopy, we'll never run.
Each funny face, we share and tease,
Joy in the air, a silly breeze.

So gather round, let's share our tales,
Of fruity capers and wild flails.
For in this dusk, we find our joy,
In laughter together, every girl and boy!

Golden Elixir

Under a tree where the shadows play,
Fruits of gold in a cheerful ballet.
Smiles light up like fireworks bright,
As the juicy surprise takes its flight.

Laughter spills from the branches near,
Sipping sweetness with each joyful cheer.
Sticky fingers and painted grins,
This feast of fun is where the joy begins.

Bellyaching giggles, a quirky sound,
The wild fruit dance spins round and round.
Chasing our giggles with every bite,
The world's a joke on a warm, merry night.

In the glow of celestial beams,
We share wild dreams served with ice cream.
Life is a fruit, oh what a jest,
Fill up your cup, let's toast to the best!

Harmony of Light and Flavor

In the garden where laughter grows,
Colorful charms in a whimsical prose.
The light chuckles, oranges blend,
With each funky twist, we shall transcend.

Bright cheeks bulge with a zesty crunch,
Tropical giggles in every munch.
Swinging from vines, oh what a sight,
Flavors dancing in the warm moonlight.

Joking with shadows that leap and spin,
Chasing the taste, that cheeky grin.
Whispers of joy beneath the stars,
As we feast and dream in this land of bars.

Lemonade lakes and laughter streams,
A concoction of fun fills our wild dreams.
Every sip drips with a cheeky flair,
Sharing our secrets, we float in the air.

Citrus Sighs

In the orchard where the mischief thrives,
Zesty peels and butterfly dives.
With a wink, a twist, and a silly sound,
We play like fruit in the fun we found.

Giggling tides wash over us bright,
With candied laughter spilling the night.
The taste so sweet, it gives a cheer,
Ticklish kisses from the fruit we revere.

Fruits juggling joy, a lively scene,
Squeezed into smiles that twinkle and gleam.
Banana slips and high-flying dreams,
In this playful place, nothing is as it seems.

Echoes of fruity hymns in the breeze,
Dancing with joy like the rustling leaves.
Infinite giggles, we roll on the ground,
In this jolly orchard, pure magic is found.

Night Song of the Tropics

Beneath the stars, where the rhythms play,
Juicy jests spin the night away.
Glow of laughter in the breezy air,
We chase the giggles without a care.

Fragrant whispers, a fruity delight,
Teasing the senses till morning light.
Bubbly bursts in the playful dark,
The night is alive, igniting the spark.

Frolicking spirits dance on the sand,
Silly conquests led by the band.
Zesty tunes lift us high and free,
In this tropical night, just you and me.

A chorus of joy, our hearts in sync,
With each little taste, we laugh and wink.
So, raise a toast with a cheeky grin,
In this playful night, let the fun begin!

Sonder Beneath the Stars

Under the glow of night's delight,
We dance with shadows in soft flight.
Laughter bubbles like fizzy soda,
While twinkling stars play peekaboo moda.

Jupiter's winks, a cosmic joke,
We giggle under the night's smoke.
A whispered secret, then a snort,
As crickets hold their funny court.

Fat squirrels navigate their dream,
Chasing fireflies in a gleam.
In every chuckle, there's a spark,
A serenade from the midnight park.

We sip our drinks, the flavors tease,
While sleepy cats stretch in the breeze.
Tonight, we're light, like paper planes,
Crafting joys that know no chains.

Honeyed Celestial Tides

Moonbeams dip in the honeyed sea,
We splash and giggle, oh so free!
With every wave, a joke takes flight,
As seaweed dances, a silly sight.

The starfish chuckle, a crusty band,
As we narrate tales, unplanned.
Crabs applaud in the sandy ring,
Cheering us on, as we sing!

Each splash a story, each wave a grin,
The tide rolls in, let the fun begin!
We ride the currents, laughter swells,
Echoing laughter, our secret spells.

Drifting under an ocean sky,
We dream of jellyfish flying high.
With sticky toes and hearts so light,
We bask in fun till morning light.

Fleeting Twilight Bliss

In twilight's grasp, we find our cheer,
As fireflies buzz, their glow sincere.
We chase shadows, a merry race,
With laughter bubbling, setting the pace.

A wayward breeze, a wandering hat,
Sends us spinning in playful combat.
With every tumble, giggles grow,
As stars peek in, putting on a show.

We share our dreams, like candy flung,
As crickets hum their softest song.
Forget the worries of the day,
Tonight's a treasure, come what may.

Beneath the blush of sky so bright,
We wrap our joys in soft twilight.
Each fleeting moment, sweet as pie,
These giggles and grins will never die.

Tropical Reflections

Beneath the palms, our laughter flows,
With coconut dreams and flip-flop toes.
The breeze is teasing, like playful kittens,
As we spin tales that leave us smitten.

Banana peels in a comedic dance,
While surfboards mimic our silly stance.
We dive for joy in the sparkling bay,
Catching giggles that drift away.

A sunset blushes, a fruity hue,
We sip our drinks, tasting joy anew.
With cada kokos, our worries release,
We bounce like waves, embracing peace.

In this tropical mirth, life's a parade,
With friends and fun, we're never afraid.
These sun-kissed moments, forever bright,
A canvas of laughter, in pure delight.

Lush Gardens of Stillness

In gardens where the fruit trees sway,
A monkey with a hat came to play.
He danced with joy, a funny sight,
While chasing fireflies through the night.

A parrot perched upon a vine,
Sipped juice and acted quite divine.
With every gulp, he squawked a tune,
Underneath the glowing moon.

The crickets chirped, their legs did tap,
As laughter echoed, not a nap.
A tortoise joined with comic flair,
It took him ages—was he there?

Then suddenly, a cat passed by,
With dreams of fish drifting on high.
He tripped on roots, oh what a sight,
And rolled away into the night.

A Ballad of Tropic Dreams

Beneath the palm, where shadows scheme,
    A lizard plots his tropical dream.
    He wears a crown of shiny green,
    And claims the title of the queen.

A tidal wave of giggles swells,
    As rhythmic waves tell silly tales.
    With every crash, a splash unfolds,
    And secrets of the ocean's gold.

The seagulls joke and dive in jest,
    Each thought they were the very best.
    A crab retorts with sideways pride,
    And all the fish just laugh and hide.

Yet in the dusk, with colors rife,
    A sandman's built with all his life.
    But when a wave washed him away,
    He waved goodbye and told the bay.

Sunlit Glimmer Amidst Twilight

The sun dipped low in skies of pink,
A pig danced round the pond to think.
With floppy ears and twinkling eyes,
He swirled and spun, much to our surprise.

A rabbit joined, with hops so fleet,
Both tripped and landed near my feet.
They laughed aloud, what a silly sight,
As stars emerged from deepening night.

With glowworms lighting up the scene,
They formed a chorus, quite a team.
Each note they sang, a funny quirk,
As nature laughed, no one did shirk.

Then came a frog, with poetry grand,
Who recited rhymes in a rock band.
The crickets joined with string and drum,
And played until the morning's hum.

Echoes of Warmth and Wonder

In twilight's glow, a sneaky fox,
Wore socks on both his furry paws.
He tiptoed by the glowworm's show,
And giggled as he made them glow.

A rabbit wore a top hat, too,
He danced around, said 'look at you!'
The forest chuckled in delight,
As creatures sparkled in the night.

Then down the path, a raccoon pranced,
With shiny jewels—oh, how he danced!
He wore them all, unmatched in flair,
While crows passed by with stares to spare.

But when the dawn began to rise,
They hastily retreated, no surprise.
In whispers, warmth and wonder cling,
And echoes fill the air with zing!

Fragrant Hues Under the Night

In the garden, laughter flows,
A fruit tree struts in silly shows.
Wobbling branches, a breeze so light,
Crispy leaves dance, a comical sight.

A squirrel issues a cheeky dare,
To pluck a treat high in the air.
But every jump turns into a flop,
As he tumbles down with a silly pop.

Sticky fingers, oh what a waste,
"Is this dessert, or a messy paste?"
Friends giggle under the starry sky,
As juicy bites make the laughter fly.

With each nibble, the night becomes bright,
Chasing fireflies, what a joyful sight.
The moon peeks down with a cheeky grin,
As we feast like kings, let the fun begin!

Dreaming of Sun-Kissed Shores

On a beach where the sun loves to play,
A crafty crab runs in a funny ballet.
With flip-flops on, I feel quite grand,
But I trip on sand with my awkward stand.

I spot a snack, bright as the sun,
But seagulls swoop, oh what have they done?
A sandwich flutters into the blue,
As I stand shocked, with a skyward view.

On surfboards we paddle, giggling with glee,
While waves splash loudly, wild as can be.
The sun sets golden, painting the shore,
With laughter echoing, who could ask for more?

As night blankets softly, stars pop awake,
We dance with shadows, making mistakes.
With silly grins and sand on our toes,
We sing to the moon, as the ocean glows!

A Symphony of Radiance

In the garden, a fruit band plays,
With giggles echoing in radiant rays.
Lemon drums thump, and oranges sing,
While berries waltz in a bright, mad fling.

The night is a show, full of cheer,
As fruits put on coats of gold, my dear.
"Who's the juiciest?" they cleverly tease,
While I'm dodging peels and sticky trees.

A pumpkin jives, all round and plump,
While carrots leap, giving a jump.
In this bizarre orchestra, what a delight,
Where laughter fills up the giggly night.

With twirling tunes, clinks, and clatters,
Even in chaos, joy surely matters.
So raise a toast to this comical spree,
Where every bite flavorfully sways free!

Moonlit Orchard's Embrace

Under the glow of a glowing sphere,
The orchard's secrets whisper near.
With cheeky apples in playful rows,
And pears holding jokes only they know.

A raccoon juggles fruit with flair,
I gasp in shock, how does he dare?
"Don't drop that peach, you little fool!"
While I laugh at his clumsy school.

Beneath the leaves, shadows skitter,
As fruit bats dance, getting glitter.
Each flutter brings a fresh surprise,
With silly antics 'neath bright night skies.

We munch and crunch, what a joyful race,
With laughter bouncing all over the place.
The orchard awakens with giggles galore,
In this moonlit haven, who could ask for more?

Tales of the Summer Night

In the garden so bright, with lanterns aglow,
A fruit fell from the tree, with a splat and a show.
We laughed till we cried, as it rolled down the lane,
Sticky hands and silly hats, who needs the rain?

Fireflies danced, mischief in their flight,
Caught a bug in a jar, not a clue in their sight.
We opened the lid, what a buzzing alarm,
The party grew louder, oh, it had its charm!

Friends with faces covered in juice, what a sight,
Trying to catch laughter under the moonlight,
With hiccups and giggles, we sang silly tunes,
As nectar dripped down, like sugary loons.

The night spun around, like a fruity delight,
We cheered for the harvest, what a wondrous bite.
Handfuls of joy, we counted our loot,
In the tales of the summer, sweet moments take root.

Glow of the Sun-Kissed Fruit

Underneath the canopy, the silliness reigned,
We discovered a fruit, incredibly stained.
With faces like goblins, and sticky delight,
We tossed it like baseballs—oh, what a sight!

Beneath the bright stars, our laughter took flight,
Chasing runaway fruit, oh, what a wild night!
We slipped and we slid in the soft golden grass,
The sun-kissed treasure left marks, oh alas!

With each funny moment, the hours flew by,
As our fruit-fueled antics made us sigh.
In the glow of our joy, all worries took flight,
We danced till we dropped in the cool of the night.

So let's raise a toast to the fruit that we found,
With giggles and glee, together we drowned.
In the laughter of summer, we'll always remember,
The nights full of fun, like a warm glowing ember.

Radiance in the Twilight

As the sun waved goodbye, the laughter began,
We summoned a fruit, so odd, yet so grand.
Just a playful toss, and it flew through the air,
Boom! It hit a neighbor, oh my—beware!

With giggles and snickers, our secret we kept,
The fruit-throwing game left all of us swept.
We giggled and plotted like pirates at sea,
Each splat brought more laughter, how funny to be!

The moon overhead watched as we took our stand,
With juice on our faces, we made a grand band.
We sang silly songs, as our bounty lay strewn,
Turning night into music, beneath the bright moon.

So here's to the fun, in the twilight we trod,
With fruits thrown like laughter, no chance to be flawed.
The radiance of joy upon each merry face,
Made summer nights lively in this laughter-filled place.

Beneath the Silvery Glow

Beneath the silvery glow, a ruckus was made,
With fruit juice as weapons, a grand masquerade.
We took aim at each other, oh what a fun game,
The ground looked like art, with our colorful claim!

We broke into fits, as we slipped and we slid,
Our dancefloor turned sticky, oh boy, what a kid!
As we rolled in the grass, we thought we were sly,
But the laughter echoed, as the fruit zoomed by.

In secretive whispers, we hatched silly plans,
What fun to concoct with sticky, sweet hands!
We crafted a story, with each juicy fling,
Underneath the soft sparkle, how happiness sings!

So here we shall laugh 'neath the beautiful night,
With memories crafted in fruit-flavored light.
Beneath the silvery glow, friendships shall bloom,
In the fruity adventure, banishing gloom.

Star-Kissed Orchard

Under the night sky, fruits dance in cheer,
Chasing away worries, drawing us near.
With giggles and laughter, we twirl like the breeze,
The stars are our audience, as we laugh and tease.

A moonbeam spills giggles, splashing on trees,
While critters join in, swaying with ease.
Sticky fingers and smiles, oh what a sight,
In this fruity wonder, everything feels right.

The branches sway gently, a rhythm so sweet,
We munch on delights and shuffle our feet.
As the laughter echoes, the night wears its crown,
In this orchard of joy, we dance up and down.

With a wink and a smile, we pluck and we munch,
A feast under starlight, we savor the crunch.
Even the crickets tap along with our fun,
As the fruit bids goodnight, singing, "Aren't we spun?"

Juices of the Evening Breeze

A breeze whispers secrets to trees standing tall,
Juices overflowing, ready for all.
We take a wild sip from nature's own flask,
With sticky-sweet giggles, we forget how to bask.

As dusk adds some drama, we set up the scene,
A gathering of friends, each one a keen bean.
We sip from the colors, laughing out loud,
Fruits in our hair, we're a silly crowd.

The juice runs like rivers, we splash and we play,
Dancing like dolphins that glide on the bay.
With each sip we tumble, as giggles take flight,
Our drinks fizz with laughter, what a funny night!

We toast to the flavors that bubble and burst,
In this wacky, zany, delightful first.
So raise your glasses high, let the fun unfurl,
In this juice-filled wonderland, we twirl and swirl.

Golden Glow of Nightfall

When night falls with laughter, a glow fills the air,
We gather our friends, no time for a care.
In the twilight banquet, we share silly tales,
Golden delights twinkling, like freight-train gales.

The shadows grow long, but our spirits won't fade,
We feast under beams that dance, don't be afraid.
With every sweet bite, a giggle will rise,
Golden moments of joy, catch them, they fly!

We juggle and stumble, a festival's style,
With juice on our cheeks, we toast with a smile.
The fruits may go soft, but we're ready, we cheer,
As laughter fills gaps, night's own cavalier.

So here's to the fun, the golden delights,
In this chortling revelry, we indulge the nights.
Under the glow of our silly brigade,
With giggles and guffaws, we dance unafraid.

Shadows of Exotic Ripeness

In the shadows we frolic, counting stars with delight,
Exotic flavors dance, a whimsical flight.
We gamble on sweetness, like children at play,
With every ripe morsel, we laugh all the way.

The night sky is winking, the breeze holds a jest,
In fruity adventures, we're never at rest.
With guffaws that echo, we swing through the air,
Selfies with shadows, showing off flair.

A treasure of colors, we munch with delight,
Sipping pure silliness, grasping the night.
With crickets as chorus, our spirits ascend,
In this funny orchard, there's joy without end.

We spin like the shadows, wrapped up in our glee,
Under this lavish canopy, just you and me.
So gather your laughter, let it take flight,
In the shadows of sweetness, we revel tonight!

Celestial Fruit and Serene Skies

In the garden where stars play,
A luminous orb leads the way.
Fruits in giggles hang on trees,
Whisper secrets with the breeze.

Bouncing like a rubber ball,
Ripening dreams that never stall.
Between the laughter of the leaves,
Tell me, what mischief it weaves?

When night falls and giggles rise,
An orchard ripe with silly pies.
A cosmic dance of fruit and joy,
Night's banquet, oh, what a ploy!

So let us twirl beneath the beams,
And feast upon our zesty dreams.
With stars above and joy in hand,
We'll celebrate this jolly land.

Nectarous Secrets Unveiled

Underneath a shining sphere,
The garden's laughter draws us near.
With every sip of tasty cheer,
The night reveals what we hold dear.

Sweet nectar drips from every bite,
A dance of flavors, pure delight.
It tickles tongues and sets us free,
In this zany jubilee!

So we gather round, oh what a sight,
With goofy grins and hearts so light.
Each fruit a tale, a comic scheme,
What could be wilder than this gleam?

And in the end, with smiles wide,
We toast to joy and laughter's ride.
For secrets sweet and laughter bold,
In midnight orchards, life unfolds.

Enchanted Orchard at Midnight

A glow hangs low in the soft, cool air,
While critters gather with funny flair.
In trees that giggle and sway like fools,
Whimsical fruits break all the rules.

Under the spell of a twinkling star,
We chase the dreams that wander far.
Each bite is magic, ripe with jest,
As midnight munchies become our quest.

Silly shadows dance on the ground,
In this orchard where laughs abound.
With every peel, a chuckle bursts,
In the fruiting laughter, we quench our thirsts.

So come and join this midnight spree,
Where mirth and mischief roam so free.
In this enchanted slice of night,
We're scooping joy with pure delight.

The Gathering of Warmth and Light

In the whispers of the evening glow,
We gather here, let laughter flow.
With warm, sweet fruits both bold and bright,
We celebrate this joyful night.

The golden hues dance on our cheeks,
As playful smiles exchange our peaks.
Oh, what joy, what silly games,
In the dance of fruit, we all proclaim.

When shadows play and bright stars beam,
We blend our dreams with mirthful schemes.
Each laugh a glow, each cheer a spark,
In this fruit-lit joy, we leave our mark.

So grab a slice, and let's delight,
In this gathering of warmth tonight.
With every chuckle, every bite,
We paint the world in colors bright.

Night's Sweet Cravings

Under the stars, a fruit parade,
Stumbling on joy, in moonlight wade.
Dancing with shadows, a playful spree,
Laughter and sweetness, just you and me.

Bouncing around like silly fools,
Chasing the laughter, breaking all rules.
Sipping on giggles, we twirl and glide,
In this sweet jest, we take our ride.

The breeze carries whispers, cheeky and bold,
While fruity delights, in stories unfold.
With every chuckle, we savor the night,
In this amusing feast, everything's right.

So here's to the moon, funky and bright,
Shining on pleasures, oh what a sight!
Every sweet bite, with laughter we chase,
In this wild dreaming, we find our place.

Aromatic Shadows

Twinkling lights and a zesty smell,
Aromas dance; they weave a spell.
With every chuckle, the shadows sway,
In laughter's embrace, we'll surely stay.

Fruit flies buzzing, they join the fun,
In this chaotically sweet run.
Joking and laughing, no reason to frown,
We'll wear our goofy hats, smile like a clown.

Tasting the night, fruits drip and spill,
With every nibble, we giggle and thrill.
A fragrant delight, the shadows hum,
In this wacky world, come join the fun.

So let's toast the night, with silly cheer,
Where the fruity magic draws us near.
Under the stars, we'll forever roam,
In this wacky adventure, we find our home.

Echoes of Eden

In a realm where giggles brightly bloom,
Under the stars, dispelling gloom.
Laughter rings out, our voices soar,
Among the sweet fruits, we'll always explore.

Ticklish breezes rustle the leaves,
As silly banter weaves through the eaves.
What's that? A fruit fight? Let's engage!
In this joyful chaos, we set the stage.

Whispers of sweetness, they call our name,
Each bite brings laughter; never the same.
As echoes of joy fill the luscious air,
We dance with abandon, free without care.

So let's gather round, in joyous parade,
Where life's a joke and worries fade.
With every chuckle, our spirits will rise,
In this garden of laughter, where every heart flies.

Harvesting Dreams

Under the glow of the silvery sheen,
We gather our dreams, sweet and serene.
Each chuckle a treasure, that's ours to keep,
With fruity delights, our laughter runs deep.

Tumbling through grass, we roll and slide,
In this game of joy, we take each stride.
Fruit baskets overflowing, what a sight!
With each little stumble, we spark pure delight.

Sipping on giggles, we feast with glee,
Chasing the echoes, it's you and me.
As flavors collide, and silliness reigns,
In this riot of joy, we break all chains.

So here's to the harvest, with friends all around,
In this whimsical journey, pure joy is found.
With each fruity burst, and laughter that sings,
We dance through the night, like playful springs.

Radiant Fruit of Dusk

Underneath the big round bliss,
A critter whispers, 'Here's the twist!'
The fruit got jiggles, what a sight,
Dancing wild in the soft moonlight.

With every bounce, a chuckle's heard,
As fruit and laughter fly, undeterred.
Little feet scamper, and they cheer,
What a fruity party, come and hear!

A squirrel in shades joins the fun,
Flipping fruits, he's never done.
The vines turn to a trampoline,
Where joy is high and grins are seen.

And when the night wraps all so tight,
The fruits shine bright, what pure delight!
A fruity ruckus, giggles soar,
The laughter echoes, who could ask for more?

Silhouettes Beneath Sunlit Night

Beneath the glow of twinkling stars,
A gang of fruits host wild bizarre.
They wear top hats, disguises cool,
Quite a party, let's not be a fool!

A banana slipped in golden shoes,
Danced with berries, what funky moves!
Jokes float high like the evening breeze,
As fruit-filled laughter brings us ease.

An orange spills secrets, juicy and sweet,
While grapes jive in their tiny feet.
They joke about the sunlight's fuss,
"Oh, how it mocks, we're glittered thus!"

Moonbeams snicker as shadows play,
The fruits unite, hip-hip-hooray!
A party not of woes or strife,
Just silly fruits living the night life!

Citrus Serenade in Twilight

As twilight falls, the fruit brigade,
Makes a serenade, a funny parade.
Lemons in tuxes, limes dress fine,
Composing tunes with a zesty line.

Bouncing tunes with a citrus twist,
Dancing twirls, no chance to resist!
With every beat, they brighten the gloom,
A fruity frenzy just starts to bloom.

A pomelo sings in a high, sweet key,
While cherries laugh with such glee.
Let's toast to fruits, so bright, so loud,
In this sunset show, we're all so proud!

The stars above wink with delight,
As fruits groove on throughout the night.
With melodies sweet, the laughter flows,
A citrus choir, as the evening glows!

Sweetness in the Twilight Glow

As daylight fades, the fruits awake,
With sweet discussions and fun to make.
Strawberries giggle, teasing the pear,
"Oh, you look ripe, let's comb your hair!"

The nighttime brings a silly shock,
As tiny fruits begin to talk.
Pineapple's crown spins round and round,
While blueberries burst out with a sound.

Cackles soar from fruit-infused brains,
Jests bounce off the sugar canes.
"I'm sweeter!" claims the juicy peach,
The laughter rings, it's within reach.

Under the softest, shimmering shade,
They spark joy like a fruit parade.
In the twilight, fun doesn't cease,
Just silly fruits seeking a piece!

www.ingramcontent.com/pod-product-compliance
Lightning Source LLC
Chambersburg PA
CBHW060114230426
43661CB00003B/179